South Australia's Natural Landscapes
The Journey Continues

Text by Cil and Pete Dobré
Photography by Pete Dobré

Acknowledgements

Our sincere thanks goes to the following people, for their support and assistance, allowing us to bring this beautiful photographic journey to you. Thank you:

- Jane McLean from Jane McLean Design for your amazing patience, thoroughness and high standard of work.

- CMI Southside Service Department and mechanics, especially Rick Pilkington for your meticulous maintenance of our Toyota vehicle.

- The Bridgestone Team and Stanley Toh, for your valued support and trustworthy product. We have safely travelled for over 12 years with Bridgestone.

- Greg Moore and the Adelaide team at TJM Products for your support, products and expert advice.

- Steve Lewis and the team at The Bureau, for your help and unhesitating involvement in this book. Special thanks to Rick Hurren for your patience and attention to detail, as we strive for excellence.

- Fuji Australia for the superb fine grain film and colour saturation.

- Maxwell Optical Industries Pty Ltd for the combination of Nikon cameras and lenses. They are a pleasure to use, displaying outstanding quality.

- Gwenda Steward (Cil's mum) for her willing and tireless efforts editing our work.

National Library of Australia Cataloguing-in-Publication Data:
Dobré, Pete, 1958-
South Australia's Natural Landscapes: The Journey Continues.
ISBN 1 920822 03 8
1. Landscape photography - South Australia.
2. Natural history - South Australia - Pictorial works.
3. South Australia - Pictorial works. I. Title.
779.369423

Published and distributed by Pete Dobré's Oz Scapes
P.O. Box 305, Happy Valley, South Australia, 5159, Australia
Email: ozscapes@cobweb.com.au   Phone/Fax: +61 8 8381 5895
Website: www.petedobre.com
Photographs copyright © 2003 by Pete Dobré
Text copyright © 2003 by Cil and Pete Dobré

Printed in Hong Kong

Front Cover: Cobb & Co. Cottage near Burra,
Remarkable Rocks, Pennington Bay, Murray River
Title Page: Bunyeroo Valley, Flinders Ranges

In 'The Journey Continues,' we have presented different areas in South Australia's tourism regions, compared to our first book. Different images of Wilpena Pound, Flinders Ranges and Remarkable Rocks, Kangaroo Island, have been included again, as they are major icons of South Australia.

Behind every act of creation lies the Creator.

Photographic Books by Pete Dobré

The Barossa,
South Australia

South Australia's Natural Landscapes

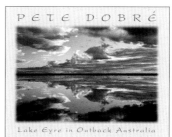
Lake Eyre in Outback Australia

Port Campbell National Park,
Victoria

The Simpson Desert
in Outback Australia

The Flinders Ranges,
South Australia

The Strzelecki, Birdsville &
Oodnadatta Tracks in
Outback Australia

Adelaide, South Australia

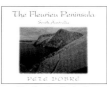
The Fleurieu Peninsula,
South Australia

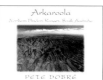
Arkaroola, Northern Flinders
Ranges, South Australia

The Cooper Creek in the
Australian Outback

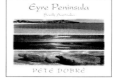
Eyre Peninsula, South Australia

Kangaroo Island, South Australia

Foreword

Pete Dobré is a downright brilliant photographer. He and his team — wife/chief organiser/writer Cil and rainbow spotters/pack mules/apprentice landscape freaks/children Jed and Tess — are delightful South Australians in love with our rich mosaic of a state. And so it was a pleasure to be asked to introduce this second superb collection of hard-earned photographs.

Then came the pain. As we are constantly reminded on our story telling trips for our Postcards TV show, a picture is still worth a thousand words. In Pete's case, they are so eloquent that any introductory scribblings would be as grains of sand in one of his Yorke Peninsula seascapes. Allow me, then, some humbly offered thoughts about how these images came about and why they are so powerful in my eyes.

As you browse, you will surely share the sense that Pete searches for these frozen moments with a passion verging on the ridiculous. What else explains his last minute urge to drive a thousand kilometre round trip just to experience and capture a total eclipse? (By the way, the two shots in this volume are the only two he recorded. His camera was inexplicably jammed for most of the twenty-six seconds available.) In another example of his devotion, the rare at-home-with-a-Wedge-tailed-Eagle shots involved ten different trips to Orroroo and tricky climbs up a tree. It is a film consuming passion as well. Over five years and a bit, Pete has shot somewhere near 15000 photos to bring us the 150 or so in the book.

The chosen few reveal that he has the jeweller's gift of dramatizing familiar gems like the red cliffs of Ardrossan and a back road in the Barossa Valley. He also has the landscape master's sense of perfect positioning that excites us into making our own tracks down roads less travelled to experience places undiscovered. Their accumulative effect reinforces my personal observation and sense of gratitude that has steadily grown through our own TV meanderings. It is increasingly clear this vast chunk of the continent is a cornucopia of landscapes that are timeless — still largely untouched and undiminished by human hand.

Pete and family would argue, of course, that nature is no accident at all, and that he is simply capturing God's design. Regardless of our own spiritual persuasion, we can all share not only his elation, but also his sense of personal insignificance in the vast cosmos.

'South Australia's Natural Landscapes – The Journey Continues' is a wonderful collection of visual psalms, enjoyable and important on a number of levels. Let them engulf you. And make you think. And most of all inspire you. I just love them.

Keith Conlon, *Postcards, NWS 9*

Appreciation

When viewing our work, please realise this isn't just the work of Pete Dobré, but the whole family. Without the support of Cil, Tess and Jed, Oz Scapes could not function.

I'm thankful for my awesome wife and my best mate, whose supportive and active role in Oz Scapes allows us to continue blazing the trail. Without her love of the outdoors and life in a tent, leaving comforts behind, our work would not be possible.

People see Pete Dobré as the man behind the images. Yet in order for Oz Scapes to exist, there is continuous, demanding and complex work behind the scenes. Without this, the images would remain as transparencies in a file. Cil is the 'engine room,' with overwhelming commitment to Oz Scapes. Thanks mate for your wisdom, guidance and love.

Tess and Jed also play a major role. From 6 weeks of age, they blazed the trail with us, seeing life in a tent as a natural way of life. God has given Tess and Jed amazing gifts and unique personalities. It has been special watching them grow and develop in the wild places of Oz.

As a family we are entering a new era in our lives. For the first time, I am going away often on my own, due to Tess's commitment to high school.

On trips, Tess has been my consistent sunrise partner. Often Tess needed more sleep, but chose to rise early. Together we've witnessed many sunrises, seeing God work in amazing ways. As a dad, I wouldn't swap this for anything. Tess's enthusiasm, vitality and her love and understanding of God is a delight. Thanks Tess for being my companion and friend on top of the mountains.

When we arrive at a new place, Jed explores, looking for different things. I love seeing him explore. His quiet subdued nature is a delight. He is a warm sensitive lad, with a strong sense of justice and passion, stemming from his love of God. It shines out in our travels. Jed your warmth and sensitivity is rare and beautiful. Your gentle hugs and little pats on the back are everlasting memories, which money cannot buy.

Thank you Tess and Jed for accepting our crazy lifestyle, leading us to many awe-inspiring places in God's creation.

Above all, I thank God for his wisdom, plans in life, for all he has done and for giving me the most wonderful mates - Cil, Tess and Jed. As a landscape photographer, I marvel at God's creation. I can't wait to see his perfect world one day. Imagine the landscapes there!

"For everything, absolutely everything, above and below, visible and invisible......everything was created by him and finds its purpose in him." Colossians 1:16

South Australia's Natural Landscapes

South Australia is a state of wonderful variety and contrast. Located centrally in Australia, it is readily accessible from the other states.

Enjoy the contrasts - from the reds of desert dunes, to shades of white on our pristine sandy beaches and the lush green vineyards and pastures.

Observe the colours of South Australia's four seasons. Compare the vivid aqua waters on our coastlines in summer, to the deep navy blue seas rolling in on a stormy winter's day. The green vineyards of the Eden Valley in December change to red and golden shades in autumn.

Bushwalk amongst colourful wildflowers in the Flinders Ranges and on Outback tracks in spring. At the Flinders in winter, rain brings out the bark texture in the River Gums and rock faces reflect in waterholes. Rain fell heavily in winter 2001. We were amazed at the greenest Flinders we'd ever seen. The images taken were beyond our wildest imagination.

A similar situation occurred in the Outback. The dry Oodnadatta Track normally flanked by sand, dirt and rocks was lined with a vibrant green carpet, after that year's rain.

The iridescent green rolling hills in winter on the Fleurieu Peninsula and Kangaroo Island will surprise you. Return in summer when golden paddocks shimmer in the hot sun. Many states of Australia are unable to claim such seasonal landscapes.

Whether a visitor or a local, consider regional visits at various times of the year, to appreciate the beautiful seasonal changes to our natural landscapes.

Colonel Light once said that posterity would judge the way future generations respond to challenges faced by idealistic colonists. Indeed they have - turning an unknown wilderness into a pleasant place in which to live and travel. From wonderful cosmopolitan Adelaide, travel in any direction and you will reach the varied beauty, attractions, regions and natural landscapes, merely a few hours away.

Head to the Limestone Coast, with rugged limestone cliffs, pounded by the Southern Ocean and the sandy shores on tranquil beaches. You will also view pastureland and vines. On the way, visit the Coorong where over 200 species of birds live or nest among the lakes and lagoons, flanked by dunes. Visit the bird observatories and lookouts on your way. The safe beaches attract seals, dolphins and sea lions, as well as providing ideal conditions for fishing, sailing and scuba-diving. Enjoy the windswept dunes and the geometric curves and patterns, changing daily with the wind.

For a soothing restful time of contemplation, head to the Murray River. The river constantly changes, as it sweeps southwards to the Murray Mouth. Appreciate the towering River Red Gums and the dramatic limestone cliffs with birds nesting in caverns. Pull over to nearby billabongs and sprawling flood plains, where massive pelican flocks congregate on dead tree trunks. Hear the call of the birds. Rise early to see mists rolling by, the sun rising behind the trees and lighting the cliffs with an overpowering orange glow; leaving you speechless, with a strong passion for this river to be saved and protected from the serious ecological situation presently faced.

Travelling through South Australia's wine regions, from the Barossa and Eden Valleys, to the Clare Valley and the rolling valleys of the Adelaide Hills, to the Fleurieu Peninsula, Riverland and down to the Coonawarra in the Limestone Coast region, the number of vineyards cropping up in the South Australian landscape will surprise you. Vineyards are replacing pastureland. The contoured and variegated patterned hills of vineyards accompany hilly backdrops, Eucalyptus trees or rolling coastline. From the air,

the graphic interfacing paddocks form amazing images of this industry which makes South Australia famous internationally.

We always feel excited when we visit Kangaroo Island, Australia's third largest island. Aqua waters, jagged rocks, white sandy beaches (including Vivonne Bay - named Australia's best beach in 2002), crashing waves, vivid green hills - so many picturesque scapes! We met an overseas tourist who aptly described the island. This living natural history museum, teeming with wildlife, was called 'a big zoo without cages' - a beautiful interpretation of the wildlife, living naturally in this piece of paradise, from Rosenberg's sand goannas, Cape Barren geese, koalas, kangaroos, echidnas, Little Penguins to the Australian sea lions.

Visit the Fleurieu Peninsula to bushwalk, whale watch, participate in a variety of water sports and enjoy fine local produce and wines. The sweeping views over grassy hillsides, patterned vineyards and lush dairy country covered in gums, will delight you, as you travel the winding roads leading to the beautiful coastline.

Reaching Yorke Peninsula, you travel through remnants of once prosperous mining towns, past classic homesteads and miners' cottages, to reach picturesque cliffs and sandy beaches. You may dive on a shipwreck, one of many which dot the coastline. Choose surfing in Innes National Park and its surrounds, or enjoy a fishing charter. Anglers, surfers and bushwalkers love this natural scape, just three hours from Adelaide.

Further on you see some of Australia's best beaches and fishing spots amongst the rugged scenery on Eyre Peninsula. You may surf at many beaches, including the highly acclaimed Cactus Beach. Swim with dolphins and sea lions at Baird Bay. View the only mainland colony of Australian sea lions at Point Labatt Conservation Park and watch Southern Right Whales frolicking at the Head of Bight, where every winter they come to mate and give birth. While camping, bushwalking, 4WDing or fishing on Eyre Peninsula, you will enjoy the culinary delights as commercial operators open their doors to give insight into the industry.

As you head north from Adelaide to the Flinders Ranges, enjoy abounding wildlife. Emus graze, kangaroos and Yellow-footed Rock Wallabies hop around and Wedge-tailed Eagles soar above, while flocks of galahs screech. As majestic mountain ranges thrust upwards, they are often enshrouded by early morning clouds. Then they become mysterious silhouettes in a blazing sky at sunset. As you pass derelict towns and abandoned mine shafts, they remind you of past mining and pastoral activities. Look closely at the majestic Red Gums near creek and river beds. Walk up closely to see the earthy tones and graphic patterns in the bark and texture. See varying shades of blue, green and brown in the Flinders Ranges, depending on the season.

Head further north, with its surrounds of vast horizons and dry desolate landscapes. Stony deserts, glittering and seemingly endless salt pans, vivid red sand dunes and rocky outcrops are spectacular. While skies spread endlessly, stoop down to see minute bugs and insects under rocks and shrubs.

Stone ruins gradually crumbling testify to the fickle nature of the Outback. We stop and wonder about the family history, their struggle on the land and the reason they first settled in the Outback. Fly over the Outback for a contrasting view and appreciate its extent. No wonder the South Australian Outback has earned a reputation in the International Film Industry. As dusk approaches, Outback skies turn amazing shades of red and orange, before abundant stars brilliantly shine in the night sky - always capturing our excitement.

Whether a peaceful escape to seaside scapes, exploring nautical heritage, enjoying spectacular sunsets, the legendary Outback, fine wine and food, nature, wildlife or heritage, South Australia offers something for everyone, while enjoying the scenic natural landscapes. South Australia is both diverse and stunning.

Wonder and contemplate the beauty of creation as you journey through 'South Australia's Natural Landscapes.'

* * * * *

Stories behind the photos contain the hardships, joys and triumphs that make-up the photographer's experience to gain the images. When I view other photographers' work, I always ask, 'What lies behind the photograph?' I hope you enjoy reading a selection of stories behind the following images.

The Gift

Photography is rewarding and I love working in partnership with God. Yet for every great picture, there also may be major disappointments.

Great despair and disappointment occurred recently on a field trip. For ten days I worked on a variety of scenes in one region.

An old house drew me back to the start of my photographic career, because of my deep passion for old ruins reflecting the past. Walking through the hallways, I imagine the people who lived here in homes alive with vitality. In the bedrooms, there was laughter, passion and sleep. The fireplaces gave warmth to the family central meeting place, where life's choices and decisions were often made. People endured hardships and pain during long hot summers living in these homes. Again this old house stirred a flood of memories about life of former days. (Old black and white images have the same effect. I wonder what life was like, how the owners' voices sounded and what gave them their spark in life.)

On ten days I visited the old house for sunrise and sunset. God gave me amazing skies to work with. I love his creativity reflected in the sky.

On my last day the weather was a mixture. It started sour, with windy cold conditions. Yet in the next few hours, stillness and serenity engulfed the landscape. The cloud returned and there appeared a small hole towards the horizon.

Like a young child, I waited in anticipation, expecting an awesome shot, should the sun pop out and light the old house. But the cloud moved quickly and covered the sun. I knew the possibilities could be amazing, so I kept waiting in the field. Finally, after teasing me, the sun emerged from the cloud for a very short time and from a very small opening appeared the most incredible shot that I have ever seen.

Standing for a brief moment, I knew this was a gift from God. So I decided to call this image 'The Gift.' The camera worked overtime with less than 30 seconds and then the shot disappeared. I stood alone in the field, looking at the old house and wondering how many similar scenes had the original owners witnessed. I was so excited. I looked towards the heavens and thanked God for 'The Gift.' It was amazing!

Then a gentle breeze sprang up and the freshness of the air impressed me. I stood in the field, less than three hours away from Adelaide city where people rushed about. Two worlds close together, yet world's apart.

Back in Adelaide, I left 100 films for developing over several days. In that time I continued thinking of 'The Gift.'

After collecting the films I headed for the studio, to search for 'The Gift.' Every other image seemed unimportant in comparison. After 50 rolls, it hadn't appeared so I kept checking. With five to go, I felt my stomach tightening. When I reached the final roll I was sure this was it. Alas, 'The Gift' was missing. Surely there was a mistake. I phoned the lab to explain. They searched for it, but to no avail.

So I drove back to search the field and my accommodation. I drove up with my brother-in-law, longing to be at the ruin to start my search. We drove straight to the field to walk every square centimetre around the ruin. We found nothing. I threw a roll of 120 film over the field, to see if it stood out. After several hours it was obvious that the initial roll was lost.

God gave me 'The Gift,' I lost it and my disappointment was unbearable. But the image is etched in my mind forever.

Page 12

Freezing mornings are not encouraging to early rising. At times, I feel like taking the morning off.

For this sunrise, I dragged myself out of bed. I looked at the heavy sky with no gap in the horizon. But to my surprise, the sun rose with awesome shades of light and the colours deepened.

I was glad that Cil and Tess also enjoyed this sunrise. Only the pelicans joined us. I wondered how frequently such vistas occur with no-one around to enjoy the event. When you discipline yourself to rise, you view amazing scenes.

The Eclipse - page 16

For several months there was much media hype of the pending eclipse. Countless interviews of eclipse chasers from around the world were aired.

As I travelled and listened to the interviews, I wondered about all the build up to this event and whether I should visit Lyndhurst or watch it on television. At the last moment, I decided to go and a friend accompanied me.

We arrived in Lyndhurst at 3 pm to a carnival of colourful people, with music pumping and the aroma of food. Although wind blew dust everywhere, it did not dampen the sense of expectation.

After studying maps, Scott and I decided to view the eclipse away from the crowds. So we headed 30 kilometres north-east of Lyndhurst.

The wind blew so hard, preventing the stability of the tripod and the camera. The strong vibrations would result in blurred images, even with a large lens. I filled a plastic bag with huge rocks, which I tied for security to the centre of the tripod.

Ready now, I waited for the unexpected to happen. Could it be as successful as reports of previous eclipses?

I held three polarising filters together with three ND filters up to the viewfinder, at a 45 degree angle, to enable me to watch the event, without any eyesight damage.

Suddenly the sensational eclipse occurred. I now understand why people follow this event around the world. With the landscape covered in darkness, it was like the sun and moon were suspended in a moment of time. The world seemed to stop. Colours around the moon shimmered with a radiant light: truly an emotional moment.

There were 26 seconds to photograph the eclipse. However my camera played up as I tried to capture the event. I also left the video running to record the skies darkening. The footage shows the drama with my camera, my reaction and the time taken to get another lens onto the camera. That left me time for only two shots before the eclipse ended. I wanted to push 'pause' on a remote control to hold this special moment. Had I captured anything in the two shots taken? I had to wait another two days while my images were developed.

Our return trip to Adelaide provided adventure, with countless vehicles on the highway. It appeared as a long red snake with the tail lights of the cars following the road's contours. We finally arrived home at 4.45am after 'a day at the office.'

My two shots in this book excite me as I anticipated failure, but the drive to Lyndhurst was not in vain. I saw God at his best. It was as if he was saying, "Hey Pete, you think landscapes are great. Mate, take a look at this!" I understand why people chase these events around the world.

Contrasting Seasons - pages 31, 33, 34, 40, 41, 42

These images were taken in October 2001 when the Flinders had consistent rain throughout the year, after drought gripped most of the country, with not a blade of grass seen.

In years of blazing the trail, I had not seen the Flinders Ranges so green. I wondered whether I would see the area like this again. Such greenness in South Australia's Outback adds freshness, projecting life and vitality.

Moses on the Mountain Top - page 33

My daughter Tess and I were delighted to witness this special moment.

We rose from our tent at 5.45am and looked at the sky. Sadly this morning was overcast. As Tess and I discussed the unpredictability of the morning, I suggested that she may choose to stay at camp. But Tess gladly came.

As we walked along the dirt roads to the vantage point, we continually observed the sky. Arriving at the Elder Range viewing point, the sky seemed dark and heavy, with a bitterly cold wind. Tess and I waited expectantly as the clouds tumbled along. Light shafts beamed through tiny gaps like giant spotlights, lighting the landscape. Three sets of cloud formations engulfed the top of the Elder Range.

However the sky slowly changed, with amazing cloud patterns rolling over the mountain top. Just as it cleared, dark clouds formed, choking any shaft of light.

This moving scene reminded me of Moses going up to the mountain to have a chat with God. I said to Tess, 'Mate, we will stay longer. I think God is doing something special.'

Sure enough, the skies parted and a graceful white cloud dominated the scene as it rolled and twisted over the mountain top.

When you thought it couldn't get better, God had other plans. When these clouds almost disappeared, other clouds suddenly poured in. The skies darkened, new shafts spotlighted the landscape, while the long white cloud previously seen, re-emerged. Tess and I realised we may never again see such a scene.

The Climb - page 39

One of my hardest tasks is deciding what to carry and what to leave behind, before a long hike. I am convinced I need a donkey.

I desired a shot from Rawnsley Bluff, in the Flinders Ranges, looking over the sweeping plains with the Chace Range as the background. This long hike is exhausting when carrying so much equipment. The round trip takes nine hours, including time for taking pictures. Those who have experienced this trek, know that it is unwise to carry so much gear, on many consecutive days.

Leaving at 5.45am, the skies were clear with good conditions for photography. Daily, as I reached three quarters of the incline, the weather changed. I considered heading back, but each time I pressed on and waited three hours at the top, hoping for the sky to change.

After five consecutive days of climbing I needed a rest. It wasn't a wise move, for it was difficult to tackle the climb again after a day's break. But I was determined to get the shot.

On my sixth climb, conditions seemed favourable and I finally photographed the scene. Normally I wait for the late afternoon sun to produce stronger colours, avoiding the harsh light of the midday sun. Yet in this location, I couldn't wait or I would have the long shadows of Wilpena Pound engulfing the landscape and destroying this shot.

The Waterfall - page 42

For this personal highlight, as usual I rose early, so I began to browse around in the Flinders. This was not a planned shot but a view only seen once in the Flinders Ranges during my years of blazing the trail in this region.

I chose this title because the mist from the summit of the Chace Range poured over the top like a waterfall. At a certain altitude it dissipated - an awesome scene. I sat on the hill enjoying the cloud streaming over the top.

This scene reminded me of God's love, like a caring hand pouring over us, yet stopping halfway - not smothering us, but giving the freedom to explore, think, reason and act for ourselves.

Page 59

I enjoy shooting great skies and chasing clouds. I set off at 5.30am to photograph vineyards in the McLaren Vale region.

I saw this inspiring set of clouds breaking away from the main pack and drifting towards the sea. I chased the clouds until I reached Silver Sands Beach.

Driving over 60 kilometres, back and forth, eventually I shot this image at 8.45am. As the cloud hovered over the sea, I anticipated a favourite shot. The simplicity and colours invite me to return to this beach.

Page 71

Occasionally I come across unexpected shots like this one on Kangaroo Island, while visiting clients. Leaving Seal Bay this awesome sky beckoned me to nearby Bales Beach.

Not dressed in old hiking clothes, I scrambled in the bush, climbed hills and slid back down. An hour later I was hot, sweaty and dirty. I always check all angles for a shot, but this time, I ended up taking it from my first viewing point, back on the beach where I began. So much for getting dirty!

Pages 122, 123

It was seven degrees one morning and I was excited as I camped only 100 metres from this shot. The short walk to my viewing point was a luxury. The diversity of colour in these two shots emanates from a 23 minute gap.

Why are other people's images different although taken at the same location? Nine times out of ten people visit an area at the wrong time of day. The shot on page 122 was taken 15 minutes before the sun rose. It is such a special moment at that time, for light plays a very important role in photography.

* * * * *

As you continue your journey through this book, consider these words: *"No philosophical theory which I have yet come across is a radical improvement on the words of Genesis that in the beginning God created the heavens and the earth."* C.S. Lewis.

Contents

South Australia

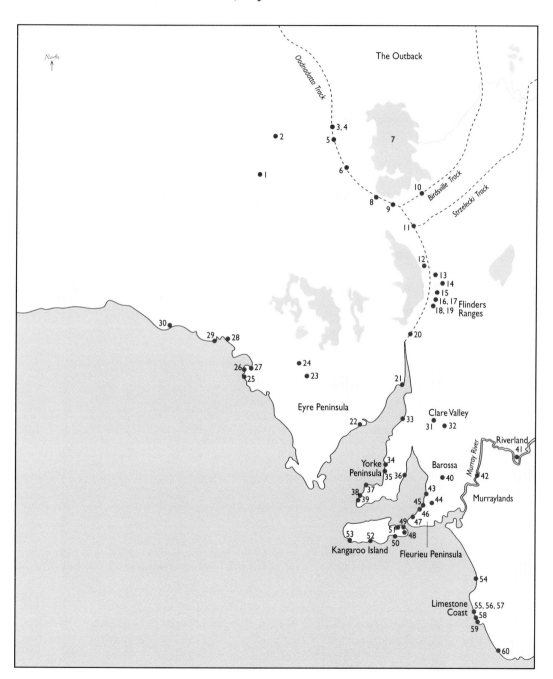

The Outback
1 Coober Pedy
2 The Painted Desert
3 Neales River
4 Algebuckina Bridge
5 Warrina Creek
6 William Creek
7 Lake Eyre North
8 Fettler's Cottage
9 Callanna Siding
10 Birdsville Track
11 Lyndhurst

Flinders Ranges
12 Nilpena Station
13 Bunyeroo Creek
14 Skytrek, *Willow Springs*
15 Wilpena Pound
16 Rawnsley Bluff
17 Chace Range
18 Arkaba Station
19 Elder Range
20 Quorn

Eyre Peninsula
21 Point Lowly Lighthouse
22 Point Gibbon
23 Mount Wudinna
24 Pildappa Rock
25 Point Westall
26 The Granites
27 Streaky Bay
28 Sandy Cove
29 Cactus Beach
30 Fowlers Bay

Clare Valley
31 Mid North
32 Burra

Yorke Peninsula
33 Port Broughton
34 The Gap
35 Balgowan Cliffs
36 Ardrossan Cliffs
37 Corny Point Lighthouse
38 Gym Beach
39 Dolphin Beach

Barossa
40 Near Rowland Flat

Riverland
41 Lake Bonney

Murraylands
42 Murray River

Fleurieu Peninsula
43 Hallett Cove Conservation Park
44 McLaren Vale
45 Silver Sands Beach
46 Sellicks Beach
47 Second Valley

Kangaroo Island
48 Chapman River
49 Penneshaw
50 Pennington Bay
51 Red Banks
52 Bales Beach
53 Remarkable Rocks

Limestone Coast
54 The Granites
55 Guichen Bay, *Robe*
56 Doorway Rock, *Robe*
57 Robe Coastline
58 Little Dip Conservation Park
59 Nora Creina
60 Carpenter Rocks

Murraylands and Riverland

Murray River

Companionship - Murray River

Murray River

Departure - Murray River

Early Morning Light – Murray River

Sunset – Lake Bonney – Murray River

Sunrise – 6.35am – Murray River

The Outback

Aerial View of The Painted Desert

Aerial View of The Painted Desert - The Outback

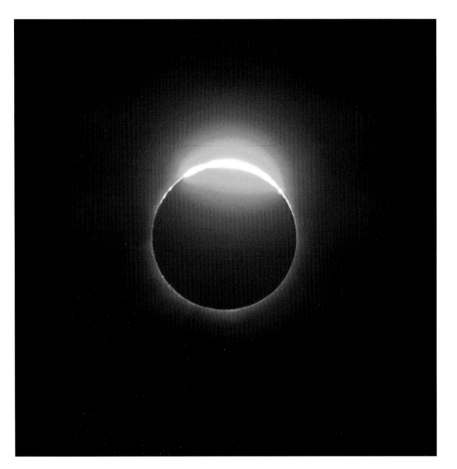

The Solar Eclipse - Lyndhurst - The Outback

Birdsville Track - The Outback

Birdsville Track after Rain - The Outback

The Neales River - Oodnadatta Track - The Outback

Callanna Siding - Oodnadatta Track - The Outback

South of William Creek - Oodnadatta Track - The Outback

Lake Eyre North - The Outback

Sand Monitor

Shingleback

The Outback

The Moon Plain near Coober Pedy - The Outback

Storm over Coober Pedy - The Outback

Aerial View of Algebuckina Bridge - Oodnadatta Track - The Outback

Algebuckina Bridge - Oodnadatta Track - The Outback

Warrina Creek - Oodnadatta Track - The Outback

Sunset at Warrina Creek - Oodnadatta Track - The Outback

Flinders Ranges

Sunrise on the Elder Range

Arkaba Station after Consistent Rain - Flinders Ranges

Bunyeroo Creek – Flinders Ranges

Elder Range - Flinders Ranges

Wilpena Pound – Flinders Ranges

Skytrek - Willow Springs - Flinders Ranges

Skytrek - Willow Springs - Flinders Ranges

Skytrek - Willow Springs - Flinders Ranges

Rawnsley Bluff Lookout overlooking the Chace Range – Flinders Ranges

Arkaba Station – Flinders Ranges

Arkaba Station - Flinders Ranges

Chace Range – Flinders Ranges

Wilpena Pound - Flinders Ranges

The Australian Windmill - Quorn - Flinders Ranges

Sturt Desert Pea – Flinders Ranges

Nilpena Station - Flinders Ranges

Looking towards Wilpena Pound from Nilpena Station – Flinders Ranges

The Blacksmith's Shop on Nilpena Station - Flinders Ranges

The Amphitheatre – Nilpena Station – Flinders Ranges

Sunset - Wilpena Pound - Flinders Ranges

Fleurieu Peninsula

Winter - Second Valley

Winter – Fleurieu Peninsula Coastline

Spring - Second Valley - Fleurieu Peninsula

Sunset - Second Valley - Fleurieu Peninsula

Winter - Second Valley - Fleurieu Peninsula

Sunset - Hallett Cove Conservation Park - Fleurieu Peninsula

Sellicks Beach - Fleurieu Peninsula

Silver Sands Beach – Fleurieu Peninsula

Barossa

Near Rowland Flat

Eucalyptus Trees in the Barossa

Autumn in the Barossa

Kangaroo Island

Sunrise - Penneshaw

Sunrise – Penneshaw Beach – Kangaroo Island

Chapman River - Kangaroo Island

God's Promise - Kangaroo Island

Sunrise - Remarkable Rocks - Kangaroo Island

Sunset - Remarkable Rocks - Kangaroo Island

Red Banks – Kangaroo Island

Bales Beach – Kangaroo Island

Pennington Bay - Kangaroo Island

Laughing Kookaburra

Koala

Kangaroo Island Wildlife

Tammar Wallaby

Brushtail Possum

Kangaroo Island Wildlife

Limestone Coast

Sunset - Doorway Rock - Robe

Sunset - Robe Coastline - Limestone Coast

Nora Creina – Limestone Coast

Nora Creina - Limestone Coast

Little Dip Conservation Park - Limestone Coast

The Granites - Limestone Coast

Guichen Bay - Robe - Limestone Coast

Carpenter Rocks – Limestone Coast

Clare Valley

Cobb & Co. Cottage at Sunset - Near Burra

Cobb & Co. Cottage at Sunset – Near Burra – Clare Valley

Approaching Storm near Burra - Clare Valley

Worn-out – Mid North

Canola Fields - Mid North

Approaching Rain - Mid North

Morphett's Enginehouse Museum at the Monster Mine - Burra - Clare Valley

Farming Land - Mid North

Wedge-tailed Eagle

Dinner Time

Yorke Peninsula

Sunrise - Corny Point Lighthouse

Sunset - Corny Point Lighthouse - Yorke Peninsula

The Gap - Yorke Peninsula

96

Balgowan Cliffs – Yorke Peninsula

Gym Beach – Yorke Peninsula

Dolphin Beach - Yorke Peninsula

Dolphins at Play - Yorke Peninsula

Port Broughton - Yorke Peninsula

Sunrise - Ardrossan Cliffs - Yorke Peninsula

Eyre Peninsula

No Longer Standing

Point Gibbon - Eyre Peninsula

Between The Granites and Point Westall - Eyre Peninsula

Between The Granites and Point Westall - Eyre Peninsula

The Granites - Eyre Peninsula

The Granites - Eyre Peninsula

Sunrise near Streaky Bay - Eyre Peninsula

Sunrise near Streaky Bay - Eyre Peninsula

Point Westall - Eyre Peninsula

Point Westall - Eyre Peninsula

Point Westall - Eyre Peninsula

Point Westall - Eyre Peninsula

Coastline West of Fowlers Bay - Eyre Peninsula

Point Lowly Lighthouse - Eyre Peninsula

Pildappa Rock - Eyre Peninsula

Mount Wudinna - Eyre Peninsula

Cactus Beach Dunes - Eyre Peninsula

Nature's Art - Cactus Beach Dunes - Eyre Peninsula

Sandy Cove - Eyre Peninsula

Sunrise – Cactus Beach Dunes – Eyre Peninsula

6.23am – Cactus Beach Dunes – Eyre Peninsula

6.46am - Cactus Beach Dunes - Eyre Peninsula

The Creator's Design - Eyre Peninsula